About this book

The Hairy Hat Man, the Kicking King, Robber Red and the Wicked Water Witch – these and all the other characters in this LETTERLAND ABC book are part of a unique teaching scheme called the Letterland Programmes.

Your children may already have met these characters in school as the System is widely used to help children learn to read, write and spell.

In LETTERLAND every letter of the alphabet is represented by a special 'pictogram' character. Each one has been carefully designed to represent the sounds which letters make in words.

Letters are abstract symbols. Children have difficulty puzzling them out so long as they remain abstract. The Letterland pictogram system was invented to give life to these symbols. It makes their behaviour in words understandable to even very small children.

The LETTERLAND ABC book introduces each of the LETTERLAND characters, and through the accompanying text emphasizes the sound that each letter commonly makes in words.

At home, children will benefit from being entertained by the characters, whether or not they have already met them at school.

This LETTERLAND ABC book and the other LETTERLAND publications are a product of the Letterland teaching programmes. They are entirely consistent with the teaching done in every school where Letterland is central to the reading curriculum.

Thomas Nelson and Sons Ltd, Nelson House, Mayfield Road, Walton-on-Thames, Surrey, KT12 5PL, UK.

51 York Place, Edinburgh, EH1 3JD, UK

Thomas Nelson (Hong Kong) Ltd, Toppan Building 10/F, 22A Westlands Road, Quarry Bay, Hong Kong.

Distributed in Australia by

Thomas Nelson Australia, 480 La Trobe Street, Melbourne, Victoria 3000 and in Sydney, Brisbane, Adelaide and Perth.

First published by Hamlyn Publishing 1985, 1987. Third and subsequent impressions published by Thomas Nelson & Sons Ltd from 1988

ISBN 0-17-410166-X

NPN 9 8 7 6 5 4

Printed and bound in Hong Kong

Letterland © was devised by and is the copyright of Lyn Wendon. LETTERLAND ™ is a registered trademark.

The Letterland school materials are published by **Letterland Ltd,** Barton, Cambridge CB3 7AY.

This book was written and edited by Lyn Wendon and Richard Carlisle

Devised and produced by Templar Publishing Ltd, 107 High Street, Dorking, Surrey.

The LETTERLAND ABC

Written by Richard Carlisle and Lyn Wendon
Illustrated by Jane Launchbury

Nelson

D id YOU know that all the letters you see in books really come from a special place called LETTERLAND?

LETTERLAND is full of people and animals who are usually invisible, because LETTERLAND is a secret place. In this book you will be able to meet them all, and see what they are really like.

There's Clever Cat, the Hairy Hat Man, and the Wicked Water Witch who causes trouble wherever she goes … and many, many more.

LETTERLAND is a wonderful place to visit. So have fun!

A nnie Apple is usually the first person you
meet when you arrive in Letterland.
She lives in an apple orchard with lots of other
apples, so she has lots of friends to play with.

Annie Apple is always very busy.
That's because apples are very important in
Letterland. Everyone needs them to put into words.

Letterland apples even have a special person to
look after them. His name is Mr A, the Apron Man.
People call him that because he uses his apron to
gather up apples for his Applestands.

Guess how many apples there are in the picture.
Do you think you could carry them all?

Annie Apple
ants
arrows

Bouncy Ben is such a busy rabbit—busy bouncing his ball and playing games, and busy bouncing into words too.

Bouncy Ben and his brothers all live in a burrow near the Letterland bridge.
Can you see one of Ben's brothers peeping out of the burrow?

Everyone likes to watch Ben playing his favourite game. It is very clever. He balances a ball on his head, right between his big, brown ears.

People say he is better at that than anyone else.
But he has to practise a lot to stay the best!
Do you think you could balance a ball on your head?

Bouncy Ben
boat
butterfly

Here's Clever Cat. She is having a picnic.
Look at all the food she has brought with her!

There are cream cakes, cucumber sandwiches
and lots of other good things to eat.
She even remembered to bring along her favourite
cushion.

Clever Cat thinks of everything! That's why people
call her Clever Cat!

She knows all sorts of things.
She knows how to cook. She knows how to cross the
road. She even knows how NOT to catch a cold.

She can also count up to a hundred.
No wonder everyone calls her Clever Cat!

Clever Cat
cream cakes
castle

Dippy Duck is always asking her duck friends round for a swim. Every day you can see them dipping and diving down at the duckpond.

Dippy Duck likes splashing about all day long… until she gets hungry, that is.

Then she dashes over to her Duck Door.
Can you see it on the other side of the duckpond?
Do you think she'll have to duck down to get through?

Guess what is waiting for her inside?
A delicious dinner of dandelions and duckweed.
It never takes her long to get that down!

Dippy Duck
daffodils
Duck Door

Eddy Elephant is not a very big elephant. But one day he's going to be EVER so big— when he grows up, that is!

Eddy enjoys doing tricks. Can you see him tossing all those Easter Eggs up in the air? Can you see which one ISN'T an Easter Egg?

When he's finished this egg trick, Eddy says he's going to eat all those eggs in eleven seconds! He couldn't be hungry after that, could he?

Eddy Elephant belongs to Mr E, the Easy Magic Man. He has taught Eddy lots of magic tricks as well. Everyone enjoys watching Eddy do those tricks. Look out for Mr E and Eddy Elephant again at the end of the book.

Eddy Elephant
eggs
envelope

Fireman Fred is the fastest fire-fighter in Letterland. In fact, one Friday afternoon Fred put out fourteen fires in five minutes.

This made him quite famous. Everyone in Letterland was so pleased that they gave him a new hose. It's a very special hose because it's full of frothy foam instead of water. So now Fred doesn't even get wet when he fights a fire.

Fortunately, Fireman Fred also knows all about Safety First. He tells the children in Letterland how to stop fires before they start. That way he makes sure he only has a few fires to fight.

Fireman Fred
frogs
fire engine

Do you like playing on a swing? Golden Girl does. She has a swing right in the middle of her garden.

Golden Girl also likes growing things—especially green grapes. When they're ripe and ready to eat, she picks them in great bunches, and loads them into her special Go-Car.

Then off she goes to give them to all the other girls and boys in Letterland. What a good girl!

Why do you think everyone calls her Golden Girl?

Some people say it's because she has the most gorgeous golden hair ... but maybe it's because she always tries to be as good as gold.

Golden Girl
grapes
goat

Everybody loves Harry, the Hairy Hat Man. He has so many hats that even Clever Cat can hardly count them all!

If you ever meet the Hairy Hat Man, remember to keep very quiet. Why? Because the only thing he really hates is noise. That's why you'll hardly ever hear him speak above a whisper.

He doesn't even wear shoes, because he says they make too much noise as he hops along.

When he's feeling especially happy, do you know what he does? He does a handstand—with his hat on!

Very quietly, mind you.

Hairy Hat Man
hairy house
horse

I mpy Ink has a very important job, because all
the children in Letterland have ink pens.
So they all need ink! Lots of it.

Sometimes Impy Ink feels extra impish. He fills his
bottle with a very special ink indeed.
It's called Invisible Ink, which means that
nobody can see it.

Impy Ink belongs to Mr I who sells all sorts of
interesting inks. He also sells ice cream.
Everyone thinks this is a very good idea, because
Mr I's ice cream tastes very, very nice!
Watch out for him again at the end of the book.

Impy Ink

ink pen

insects

Jumping Jim is Letterland's champion jumper.
He is also the best juggler in the land.
He can even jump and juggle at the same time!

Usually, you can only see one of Jim's juggling
balls because the others are moving so fast.

Every time there are jumping competitions in
Letterland, other people try to jump and juggle
as well as Jim, but no-one can. So Jumping Jim
wins every time.

Sometimes Jim jumps so high that his head
disappears in the clouds. Do you think you would
like to join him up there?

Jumping Jim
jigsaw house
jacket

The Kicking King is the best football player in Letterland. That's because he's fantastic at kicking. Sometimes he kicks his footballs so hard that they fly right across his kingdom.

Everyone in Letterland thinks they are very lucky to have such a good, kind King. He is also great fun. He loves to fly his kite, and he is very keen on pets. He has a pet kangaroo and lots of little kittens too. The kittens are not very keen on kicking, but his kangaroo is!

At weekends, the Kicking King invites everybody round to watch a Letterland football match.

They shout and cheer every time he scores a goal. Guess who keeps the score. His kangaroo?

Kicking King
kangaroo
kites

Long ago in Letterland, Lucy the Lamp Lady came to live in a lighthouse by the sea. She is called the Lamp Lady because of her smile. It is so bright and friendly that it seems to glow, and light up everything around her.

You can see the Letterland lighthouse from miles around. It is so tall that Lucy can keep a look-out from her window for anyone who loses their way. She even helps the little lambs find their way home.

Lucy the Lamp Lady watches over Letterland until late in the evening. So even when it is dark, no-one worries about getting lost. The Lamp Lady only has to smile and her lovely lemon-coloured light shines out for all to see.

LETTERLAND
LANE

Lamp Lady
lighthouse
lambs

Mm

Meet Munching Mike. He might look a bit scary, but he is not really. In fact, he is Letterland's favourite monster. He is made of metal, and he moves along on three metal wheels.

Like most monsters, Munching Mike has a mighty appetite. Can you imagine what he likes to eat for his main meal?

He munches crunchy things like motorbikes and magnets—mixed with mushy things like mashed potato and marshmallows!

Munching Mike's Mum is much bigger than Mike. So she has a much bigger appetite. In Letterland, people say she could eat a whole mountain and still have room for more!

Munching
Mike
mountains

Naughty Nick is really quite a nice boy—but nobody gets a nickname like Naughty Nick without doing something naughty to deserve it, do they? Naughty Nick just can't help being naughty now and then.

Sometimes he makes a lot of noise, just to be a nuisance. Sometimes he eats the nuts from the nut tree next door. But the naughtiest thing he ever did was with his hammer and nails. Whatever do you suppose he did?

Naughty Nick thinks that nobody will notice the naughty things he does. But they nearly always do.

How good are you at noticing things? Can you find nine of Naughty Nick's nails hidden in the picture?

Naughty
Nick
nine nails

Oscar Orange is a very popular orange. He lives in an orange box at the Letterland docks. That's where all the ships and boats come in.

Can you spot the ostrich pecking at an orange box, or the otter eating olives from a wooden crate? There is even an octopus who has just dropped in to play.

Down at the docks, Oscar Orange also has a very important friend. He is Mr O, the Old Man from over the Ocean.

All the oranges in Letterland come from over the ocean in Mr O's boat. You can see him again at the end of the book.

Oscar Orange
octopus
ostrich

Poor Peter is a playful little puppy. He loves to play in the Letterland park, but if you sometimes see him looking sad, there is a special reason. It's because he can't make his ears prick up like a police dog. Instead they droop down.
Poor Peter does not like that at all.

Poor, poor Peter! Even the penguins in the park feel sorry for him.

Poor Peter's tears run down his cheeks, plip, plop, plip, plop, and make a puddle by his paws.

Do you think, if you gently stroked his droopy ears, you could cheer him up?

Poor Peter
poppies
penguins

There are two things the Queen of Letterland loves to do. First she loves to take her umbrella with her wherever she goes. She won't be seen anywhere without it, not even in her Quiet Room.

The second thing she loves is quarrelling, so everyone calls her 'Quarrelsome Queen'.

The Queen will quarrel about anything. She'll quarrel with the Hairy Hat Man if he whispers too quietly. She'll quarrel with the King if he kicks too quickly. She is such a quarrelsome queen, she will even quarrel with a squirrel!

Quarrelsome
Queen
quilt

Robber Red is a real trouble-maker in Letterland.
He carries a sack behind his back as he runs
along.

What's in Robber Red's sack now? Roller-skates!
Rulers! A radio! He's robbed them all.
What a rascal!

People in Letterland would really like to see
Robber Red behind bars. But he runs so fast that
no-one has managed to catch him.

Sometimes, he's hard to recognise.
He makes himself look big and fat by hiding all
his stolen goods under his jumper.

But you won't let the rascal fool you, will you!

Robber Red
radio
roller skates

Now meet Sammy Snake. He always has a friendly smile on his face. Even when he hisses, no-one is scared of him.

Not all snakes love the seaside, but Sammy Snake does. He loves sunning himself by the surf and sitting on sandcastles.

Sometimes he even goes in swimming, or sailing with his friends.

Best of all, Sammy Snake likes to slither and slide about in the sand—until he gets sleepy, that is. Then he has a little snooze.

Do you think he snores when he's asleep?

Sammy Snake

sandcastle

seagull

Everyone in Letterland calls Ticking Tom 'the Teletouch Man'. That's because his job is sending messages all over the land.
Listen hard, and you'll hear him talk in tiny ticks.

Ticking Tom thinks his job is fantastic. He has a great time tinkering with telephones and tape recorders in his Teletouch Tower.

If anything goes wrong, Ticking Tom knows just how to fix it. Even if something gets tangled at the top of a tower, Tom is tall enough to reach up and put it right.

It can be a bit cloudy up that high—which is why sometimes you can't see his head.

Ticking Tom tortoises telephones

Uu

Uppy Umbrella is a happy-go-lucky umbrella. She loves to be up-and-away when the rain comes down. She doesn't mind getting wet at all. In fact, she thinks it is great fun!

Not everyone agrees with her. Do you?

Mr U, the Uniform Man, looks after all the umbrellas in Letterland. He is always extremely busy when it rains. He rushes about opening up lots and lots of umbrellas.

Luckily, all the umbrellas are as cheerful as Uppy—unless they get stuck upside down!

Uppy Umbrella
upside down
umbrellas

W hat a beautiful vase of violets!
These lovely flowers come from a valley
high up in the hills of Letterland.

Letterland violets are very special because
they have petals made of velvet.
This makes them very soft to touch, and they stay
fresh all year round.

In Letterland, all the children have violets—
especially when they are learning to count.

Count how many petals each violet has—
one, two, three, four, FIVE each!

Vase of Violets
vegetables
volcano

What a wonderful place Letterland would be if it weren't for the Wicked Water Witch.

She likes to make trouble wherever she goes. Luckily for everyone, the Wicked Water Witch isn't always very wise.

Often her best spells don't work. Once, on a winter's day, she wished she was somewhere warm, floating above the waves of a deep blue sea.

But something odd happened. Her spell whisked her off her feet and dropped her into her own Water Wells instead. Silly witch – now she's cold and very wet indeed!

Wicked Water
Witch
windmill

Xx

Two of the children in Letterland are cousins called Max and Maxine. They go to the same school and they are the best of friends.

People in Letterland call Max and Maxine the 'kissing cousins'. That's because they use a special sign to send birthday kisses to each other. It looks like two crossed lines.

Max has written this sign three times in his birthday card for Maxine. It says k-ss, k-ss, k-ss.

When Maxine sends a birthday card to Max, she likes to send many more kisses than that! Guess how many she sends.

About sixty!

Max
Maxine
fox

All the children in Letterland love playing with yo-yos. They buy their yo-yos from the Yo-Yo Man. They think that he can do the best tricks with yo-yos they have ever seen.

They always know when the Yo-Yo Man is coming because he yells at the top of his voice, 'Yo-yos for sale, bright yellow yo-yos!'.

People rush out of their houses as he yells out, 'Never say no to a yo-yo!'. Then he starts whizzing a yo-yo up and down, round and round faster than your eyes can follow.

None of the children in Letterland can make their yo-yos go so fast. Do you think you can?

Yo-yo Man
yacht
yak

Zig-Zag Zebra lives in the Letterland zoo.
This zoo isn't like an ordinary zoo.
No-one ever shuts the animals in their cages
because they are all so friendly.

Sometimes Zig-Zag Zebra pretends to be asleep
when people come to visit her. She makes a sort
of 'zzzz zzzz' sound. But she's not really asleep,
she just feels a little bit shy.

Everyone knows that Ziz-Zag is the fastest
animal in Letterland. Guess how many prizes she
has won in races.

Dozens and dozens!

Zig Zag Zebra
zoo
zebra crossing

Here are the five Vowel Men. You have already met them on other pages. Can you remember their names?

There's Mr A, the Apron Man; Mr E, the Easy Magic Man; Mr I, the Ice Cream Man; Mr O, the Old Man and Mr U, the Uniform Man.

Now you have met nearly everyone in Letterland ... but don't forget that Letterland is a secret place. That means all the people and animals are usually invisible. So when they are in words, you will only see their letter shapes.

But you'll know who they really are, won't you!

What's in the picture?

Clever Cat has spotted all these things in the pictures.
Look at each page, and see how many you can find.
With very sharp eyes you may even find more things that begin with the
same letter. If you do, Clever Cat would be very pleased!

Aa
apples
axe

Bb
balloon
bridge
bat and ball
bee
bluebells

Cc
caterpillar
crows
cottage

Dd
deer
dog
dragonfly

Ee
eclair
eleven eggs
exit

Ff
factory
flames
farm

Gg
goose
greenhouse
gate

Hh
hedgehog
helicopter
hen
holly

Ii
igloo
infant school
ink bottle

Jj
jay
jet
jogging shoes

Kk
keys
kids
kittens

Ll
ladder
lemons
lizards
logs

Mm
magnet
mouse
moth

Nn
nest
net
nettles
newspaper
nine nuts

Oo
olives
otter

Pp
palm trees
parrots
pears

Qq
question mark
quill

Rr
ruby ring
rain
river

Ss
sandwich
seaweed
spade
starfish

Tt
train
taxi
telegraph poles
telescope

Vv
valentine card
village
voles
vultures

Ww
wagtail
washing
web
wellington boots

Yy
yoghurt
yolk
Yorkshire terrier

Zz
zip
zig zag lines